Lindt

EXCELLENCE

70%
COCOA

First published in the UK, USA and Australia in
2015 by Jacqui Small LLP,
74–77 White Lion Street, London N1 9PF

First published by Larousse in 2014
© Larousse 2014

10 9 8 7 6 5 4 3 2 1

Publishing directors:
**Isabelle Jeuge-Maynart
and Ghislaine Stora**
Editorial director: **Catherine Maillet**
Art director: **Emmanuel Chaspoul**
Graphic design: **Claire Mieyeville**
Layout: **Les PAOistes**
Jacket: **Emmanuel Chaspoul
and Claire Mieyeville
with the assistance of Les PAOistes**
Production: **Vincent Hutton**
Translator: **Hilary Mandleberg**

This book has been published courtesy of
Chocoladefabriken Lindt & Sprüngli AG, Kilchberg/
Switzerland.

ISBN : 978-1-909342-95-8
© Larousse 2014

EXCELLENCE

70%
COCOA

The best ever recipes

Contents

Soft-centred chocolate cake

Serves 6–8
Preparation time: 20 min
Cooking time: 25 min

250 g (9 oz) LINDT EXCELLENCE Cocoa 70%
125 g (1 stick) unsalted butter, plus extra for
greasing • 8 eggs • 1 pinch of salt • 180 g (1 cup)
caster/superfine sugar • 50 g (scant ½ cup) plain/
all-purpose flour • icing/confectioner's sugar,
to decorate

....

1. Preheat the oven to 240°C (475°F/Gas 9).
Roughly chop the LINDT EXCELLENCE chocolate and
butter into small pieces. Melt them in a bowl in a
bain-marie, stirring frequently with a wooden spoon.
2. Separate the eggs. Add the salt to the whites and
beat until stiff.
3. In a large bowl, mix the sugar with the yolks and
beat with an electric mixer until pale in colour, light
and fluffy. Still using the mixer, beat this mixture into
the egg whites.
4. Add the melted chocolate and butter mixture.
Beat well. Gently fold in the flour, then beat again.
The mixture will reduce slightly in volume.
5. Butter a 22-cm (8½-in) diameter springform tin/
pan. Pour in the mixture and bake for 5 minutes.
Reduce the oven temperature to 150°C (300°F/
Gas 2) and cook for 20 minutes more. Check for
doneness: the blade of a knife should come out
with chocolate on it. The aim is not to cook the
mixture until dry.
6. Turn the cake out onto a wire cooling rack.
Sprinkle with icing/confectioner's sugar and
serve warm.

Chocolate fondant cake

Serves 8
Preparation time: 20 min
Cooking time: 1 hr

250 g (2 sticks) unsalted butter, softened, plus extra for greasing • 250 g (9 oz) LINDT EXCELLENCE Cocoa 70% • 3 eggs • 200 g (1¼ cups) caster/superfine sugar • 75 g (½ cup) cornflour/cornstarch icing/confectioner's sugar, to decorate

....

1. Preheat the oven to 170°C (325°F/Gas 3). Butter a 25-cm (10-in) diameter baking tin/pan and line the base with a circle of baking parchment. Butter the baking parchment. Put the baking tin/pan in a roasting tin/pan.
2. Break the LINDT EXCELLENCE chocolate into small pieces and melt it in a bowl in a bain-marie. Remove from the heat and add the butter, a little at a time, mixing well until smooth and creamy.
3. In a large bowl, beat the eggs with the sugar until pale in colour. Stir in the cornflour/cornstarch, followed by the melted chocolate and butter mixture. Mix well.
4. Pour the mixture into the prepared baking tin/pan, then pour hot water into the roasting tin/pan to reach halfway up the sides of the baking tin/pan. Bake for 1 hour.
5. Remove from the oven and leave to cool completely. Turn out and sprinkle with icing/confectioner's sugar before serving.

Tip! Make the day before to give the flavours time to develop.

Chocolate–pistachio cakelets

Serves 6
Preparation time: 25 min
Cooking time: 10 min
Chilling time: overnight

45 g (3 tbsp) slightly salted butter, plus extra
for greasing • 150 g (5 oz) LINDT EXCELLENCE
Cocoa 70% • 3 tbsp caster/superfine sugar
2 eggs • 30 g (¼ cup) plain/all-purpose flour
3 tbsp crushed pistachio nuts
For the chocolate–pistachio filling: 50 g (2 oz)
Lindt Excellence White Vanilla • 1 tbsp pistachio
paste (available online) • 1 tsp crushed pistachio nuts

....

1. The day before, make the LINDT EXCELLENCE
chocolate–pistachio filling. Break the white chocolate
into pieces and melt it in a bowl in a bain-marie.
When it is nice and smooth, add the pistachio
paste and mix well. Add the crushed pistachios
and mix again.
2. Use the mixture to fill 6 tiny silicone moulds or
use an ice cube tray. Place in the freezer overnight.
3. The next day, preheat the oven to 240°C (475°F/
Gas 9). Butter 6 small brioche moulds and cut
the remaining butter into pieces. Break the dark
chocolate into pieces and melt it in a bowl in a bain-
marie. When it has melted, add the butter and stir
until smooth using a spatula.
4. In a large bowl, mix the sugar with the eggs, add
the flour, followed by the chocolate mixture and the
crushed pistachios.
5. Use the mixture to one-third fill the brioche moulds.
Place a ball of frozen chocolate-pistachio filling
in each mould. Cover with the rest of the mixture,
then bake for 10 minutes in the preheated oven.
Serve warm.

Spiced dark chocolate pavé

Serves 8–10
Preparation time: 20 min
Cooking time: 1 hr

250 g (9 oz) LINDT EXCELLENCE Cocoa 70%
250 g (2 sticks) unsalted butter, plus extra for
greasing • 100 ml (scant ½ cup) water • 250 g
(1¼ cups) caster/superfine sugar • 75 g (⅔ cup)
plain/all-purpose flour • 3 eggs • 1 tsp vanilla
powder • 2 pinches of ground cinnamon, plus a little
extra for sprinkling • 2 pinches of green aniseed
2 pinches of ground cardamom • 2 tbsp golden rum
icing/confectioner's sugar, to decorate

....

1. Roughly chop the LINDT EXCELLENCE chocolate
and butter into small pieces. Set aside. Put the water
in a saucepan and add the sugar. Heat, stirring with
a spatula.
2. When the mixture comes to the boil, add the
chocolate, followed by the butter. Reduce the heat
and mix well. Remove from the heat.
3. Preheat the oven to 170°C (325°F/Gas 3). Put
the flour in a large bowl and add the eggs, one at
a time. Beat in the vanilla powder, cinammon, green
aniseed, cardamom and rum. Pour this mixture into
the chocolate and butter mixture and stir well.
4. Line the base of a 26 x 18 cm (10 x 7 in)
rectangular ovenproof dish or tin/pan with baking
parchment, then grease the paper. Pour the mixture
into the dish, then put the dish in a roasting tin/pan.
Pour hot water into the tin/pan to reach halfway up
the sides of the dish. Bake for 1 hour.
5. Remove from the oven and leave to cool
completely. Turn out and sprinkle with icing/
confectioner's sugar mixed with a little cinnamon
before serving.

Flourless chocolate cakes

Makes 6 small cakes
Preparation time: 15 min
Cooking time: 35 min

200 g (7 oz) LINDT EXCELLENCE Cocoa 70%
200 g (1¾ sticks) unsalted butter, plus extra for
greasing • 6 eggs • 100 g (½ cup) caster/
superfine sugar • 75 g (¾ cup) ground almonds
4 tbsp plain/all-purpose flour • flaked/slivered
almonds, to decorate • icing/confectioner's sugar,
to decorate

....

1. Roughly chop the LINDT EXCELLENCE chocolate
and butter into small pieces. Melt them in a bowl
in a bain-marie and stir until the mixture is smooth
and creamy.
2. Separate the eggs. Add the egg yolks to the
chocolate and butter mixture, then add the sugar,
ground almonds and flour. Mix well.
3. Preheat the oven to 150°C (300°F/Gas 2). Beat
the egg whites until stiff. Add 2 tbsp egg white to the
chocolate mixture to lighten it, then gently fold in the
remaining egg white, taking care not to break it up.
4. Divide the mixture between 6 greased individual
silicone moulds and bake for 35 minutes. Remove
from the oven and leave to cool slightly. Turn out
onto a wire cooling rack. Sprinkle with flaked/
slivered almonds and then with icing/confectioner's
sugar before serving.

Pizza with salted butter and chocolate caramel

Serves 6
Preparation time: 30 min
Cooking time: 11 min

250 g (9 oz) ready-made pizza dough
300 g (7 oz) LINDT EXCELLENCE Cocoa 70%
For the salted butter caramel:
25 g (1 tbsp) slightly salted or salted butter
½ lemon • 150 g (¾ cup) caster/superfine sugar
100 ml (scant ½ cup) whipping or
double/heavy cream

....

1. To make the salted butter caramel, cut the butter into pieces and put in the fridge to chill. Squeeze the lemon and strain the juice. Put the lemon juice in a saucepan over a low heat with the sugar and heat, stirring, until the sugar has dissolved. Dip a pastry brush in water and wipe it over the sides of the pan to stop the sugar sticking.
2. Meanwhile, put the cream in a heavy-based saucepan over a low heat. When the caramel has turned golden, remove from the heat and gradually add the hot cream, stirring continuously. Using a spatula, add the butter and stir until the mixture is well combined. Set aside at room temperature.
3. Preheat the oven to 240°C (475°F/Gas 9). Line a baking sheet with baking parchment. Roll out the pizza dough into a 30 cm (12 in) circle and place on the lined baking sheet. Bake for about 5 minutes.
4. Reduce the oven temperature to 220°C (425°F/Gas 7). Using a spatula, spread the caramel over the pizza dough to a thickness of about 3 mm (⅛ in) leaving a 2 cm (¾ in) caramel-free border. Roughly chop the chocolate with a knife and sprinkle on top of the caramel. Bake for 6 minutes more. Serve hot.

Chocolate-pecan barquettes

Makes 6 barquettes
Preparation time: 15 min
Cooking time: 10–15 min
Chilling time: 2 hr 30 min

1 knob of unsalted butter, for greasing • 250 g
(9 oz) sweet shortcrust pastry (bought or home-made)
175 g (6 oz) LINDT EXCELLENCE Cocoa 70%
200 ml (¾ cup) whipping or double/heavy cream
1 heaped tsp vanilla sugar • 18 pecan nuts

....

1. Preheat the oven to 200°C (400°F/Gas 6).
Butter the barquette moulds and line each with the
shortcrust pastry. Prick the bottom with a fork and
bake blind for 10–15 minutes.
2. Meanwhile, melt the LINDT EXCELLENCE
chocolate in a bowl in a bain-marie, then add
the cream and vanilla sugar. Using a spatula, mix
together until smooth and creamy.
3. Roughly chop 12 pecan nuts and distribute them
between the pastry shells. Cover with the chocolate
mixture and top each with a whole pecan nut.
4. Leave to cool at room temperature, then
refrigerate for 2 hours before serving.

Excellent idea! The barquettes are perfect for
serving at tea time or with cocktails!

Cream chocolate tart

Serves 6
Preparation time: 20 min
Cooking time: 45 min

500 g (2 cups) *faisselle* or traditional fromage
frais/cream cheese • 1 knob of unsalted butter, for
greasing • 320 g (11 oz) shortcrust pastry (bought
or home-made) • 1 vanilla pod/bean • 4 eggs
150 g (¾ cup) caster/superfine sugar • 50 g (scant
½ cup) plain/all-purpose flour • 400 ml (1¾ cups)
whipping or double/heavy cream • 1 pinch of salt
150 g (5 oz) LINDT EXCELLENCE Cocoa 70%
1 tbsp cocoa powder, to decorate

....

1. Preheat the oven to 180°C (350°F/Gas 4). Drain
the cheese in a sieve set over a bowl. Butter a 22-cm
(8½-in) diameter tart tin and line with the shortcrust
pastry. Prick the bottom with a fork and bake blind
for 15 minutes.
2. Cut the vanilla pod/bean in half lengthwise and
scrape out the seeds. Separate the eggs.
3. In a large bowl, mix together the egg yolks, sugar
and vanilla seeds. Add the flour, half the cream and
the drained cheese.
4. Add the salt to the whites and beat until stiff.
Gently fold the beaten whites into the egg and
cheese mixture.
5. Melt the LINDT EXCELLENCE chocolate in a bowl
in a bain-marie. Add the remaining cream and mix
well with a spatula until smooth and creamy. Spread
the bottom of the pastry shell with the chocolate and
cream mixture, then cover with the cheese mixture.
Bake for 30 minutes.
6. Sprinkle with cocoa powder before serving.

Tip: If you can't find "faisselle" look for a traditional-
style fromage frais or cream cheese instead.

Chocolate-praline brownies

Serves 4–6
Preparation time: 15 min
Cooking time: 20 min

150 g (10 tbsp) unsalted butter, plus extra for greasing • 180 g (6 oz) LINDT EXCELLENCE Cocoa 70% • 3 eggs • 110 g (½ cup) caster/superfine sugar • 100 g (scant 1 cup) pecan nuts, roughly chopped • 100 g (3½ oz) powdered praline (bought or home-made)

....

1. Preheat the oven to 180°C (350°F/Gas 4). Butter a 20 x 15 cm (8 x 6 in) baking tin/pan and line with baking parchment. Roughly chop the LINDT EXCELLENCE chocolate and butter into small pieces. Melt them in a bowl in a bain-marie.
2. In a large bowl, beat the eggs with the sugar and flour. Add the chocolate and butter mixture, the pecan nuts and 70 g (2½ oz) powdered praline.
3. Pour the mixture into the prepared baking tin/pan and sprinkle the surface with the remaining praline.
4. Bake for 20 minutes. Remove from the oven and leave to cool completely before cutting into pieces.

Excellent idea! This recipe combines the softness of the brownie with the crunchiness of the praline. Totally delicious!

Chocolate soufflé

Serves 6
Preparation time: 20 min
Cooking time: 25 min

6 eggs • 150 g (5 oz) LINDT EXCELLENCE Cocoa 70% • 40 g (⅓ cup) cornflour/cornstarch • 50 g (¼ cup) caster/superfine sugar • 1 knob of unsalted butter, for greasing • 1 pinch of salt • 1 tbsp cocoa powder (optional)

....

1. Separate the eggs.
2. Break the LINDT EXCELLENCE chocolate into small pieces and melt it in a bowl in a bain-marie, stirring from time to time.
3. Remove from the heat and add the egg yolks, one at a time, beating well after each addition. Sprinkle over the cornflour/cornstarch and sugar. Mix together quickly.
4. Preheat the oven to 200°C (400°F/Gas 6). Butter a 20-cm (8-in) diameter soufflé dish or 6 individual soufflé dishes.
5. Add the salt to the egg whites and beat until stiff. Add 2 tbsp of egg white to the chocolate mixture to lighten it, then gently fold in the remaining egg white, taking care not to break it up. Pour the mixture into the prepared soufflé dish and bake for 25 minutes.
6. Check for doneness: the blade of a knife should come out covered in a little of the mixture. The aim is for the inside of the soufflé to be slightly creamy.
7. Sprinkle lightly with cocoa powder, if used, and serve immediately.

Tip! If desired, you can cook these soufflés in small silicone moulds, in which case, reduce the cooking time to 15–20 minutes.

Grandma's chocolate cream

Serves 6
Preparation time: 10 min
Chilling time: 2 hr minimum

125 g (4 oz) LINDT EXCELLENCE Cocoa 70%
400 ml (1¾ cups) whole milk • 350 ml (1½ cups)
whipping or double/heavy cream • 6 egg yolks
150 g (¾ cup) caster/superfine sugar
1 level tbsp cornflour/cornstarch • 1 tsp vanilla
essence • chopped, lightly toasted pistachios,
to decorate

....

1. Grate the LINDT EXCELLENCE chocolate. Gently
heat the milk and cream together in a heavy-based
saucepan over a low heat.
2. Meanwhile, beat the egg yolks and sugar until
pale in colour, light and fluffy. Add the cornflour/
cornstarch and, still beating, add the milk and
cream mixture.
3. Pour the mixture into a clean heavy-based
saucepan over a low heat, stirring all the time until
the cream thickens. Do not allow the mixture to boil.
4. Remove from the heat and add the grated
chocolate and vanilla essence. Mix well.
5. Divide the mixture between 6 cups. Leave to cool,
then cover. Refrigerate for at least 2 hours. To serve,
sprinkle with chopped, lightly toasted pistachios.

Chocolate charlotte

Serves 8
Preparation time: 30 min
Chilling time: overnight

24 sponge fingers/ladyfingers
For the syrup: 200 ml (¾ cup) water
50 g (¼ cup) caster/superfine sugar
For the cream: 300 g (11 oz) LINDT EXCELLENCE
Cocoa 70% • 150 g (10 tbsp) unsalted butter,
softened • 4 egg yolks • 1 pinch of salt • 7 egg
whites • 60 g (⅓ cup) caster/superfine sugar

....

1. Prepare the syrup. Put the water and sugar in
a saucepan and bring to the boil. Boil for 1 minute
to dissolve the sugar. Leave to cool.
2. Pour the cooled syrup into a small bowl. Quickly
dip the sponge fingers/ladyfingers in the syrup and
use to line the bottom and sides of an 18-cm (7-in)
diameter charlotte mould. Refrigerate.
3. Prepare the cream. Break the LINDT EXCELLENCE
chocolate into pieces, add 1 tbsp of water and melt
in a bowl in a bain-marie until smooth and creamy.
Remove from the heat and add the butter, a little at
a time, stirring with a wooden spoon. Still stirring,
add the egg yolks, one at a time.
4. Add the salt to the egg whites and beat until stiff.
Beat in the sugar when the whites are stiff.
5. Add 2 tbsp of egg white to the chocolate mixture
to lighten it, then gently fold in the remaining egg
white, taking care not to break it up.
6. Pour the mixture into the sponge-lined mould and
refrigerate overnight. Unmould onto a plate and
serve immediately.

Chocolate tart

Serves 6
Preparation time: 15 min
Cooking time: approx 20 min
Chilling time: 30 min minimum

320 g (11 oz) sweet shortcrust pastry
(bought or home-made)
For the ganache: 150 ml (⅔ cup) whipping
or double/heavy cream • 125 g (4 oz) LINDT
EXCELLENCE Cocoa 70%

....

1. Preheat the oven to 170°C (325°F/Gas 3). Roll out
the pastry and use to line a 22-cm (8½-in) diameter
tart tin. Prick the bottom with a fork, then cover with
baking parchment and baking beans. Bake blind for
12 minutes.
2. Remove the baking parchment and baking beans
and cook for 8–10 minutes more. Remove from the
oven and leave to cool.
3. Meanwhile, prepare the ganache. Heat the
cream in a heavy-based saucepan over a low heat.
Break the LINDT EXCELLENCE chocolate into pieces
and melt in a bowl in a bain-marie. Gradually add
the hot cream to the chocolate, mixing well with a
spatula.
4. Fill the baked pastry shell with the ganache and
smooth the surface with a metal spatula. Refrigerate
before serving.

Chocolate coulants

Serves 6
Preparation time: 10 min
Cooking time: 8–10 min

70 g (5 tbsp) slightly salted butter, plus extra for greasing • 50 g (scant ½ cup) plain/all-purpose flour, plus extra for dusting • 200 g (7 oz) LINDT EXCELLENCE Cocoa 70% • 4 eggs • 70 g (⅓ cup) caster/superfine sugar

....

1. Preheat the oven to 220°C (425°F/Gas 7). Butter 6 individual moulds, then dust with flour. Roughly chop the LINDT EXCELLENCE chocolate and butter into small pieces. Melt them in a bowl in a bain-marie and stir until smooth and creamy.
2. In a large bowl, beat the eggs and sugar. Add this mixture to the chocolate and butter mixture, then add the flour.
3. Divide the mixture between the prepared moulds and bake for 8–10 minutes. Turn out and serve immediately.

Tips! Take care when baking the mixture that it stays runny in the middle. You can bake these coulants in individual silicone moulds if you like; it's still a good idea to grease the moulds lightly to ensure the coulants can be turned out without risk of sticking.

Dark chocolate crème brûlée

Serves 8
Preparation time: 15 min (over 2 days)
Cooking time: approx 45 min
Chilling time: overnight

200 g (7 oz) LINDT EXCELLENCE Cocoa 70%
8 egg yolks • 180 g (scant 1 cup) caster/superfine
sugar • 500 ml (2 cups) whole milk • 500 ml
(2 cups) whipping or double/heavy cream
demerara/turbinado sugar, to finish

....

1. Start the crème brûlée the day before it is
required. To make the chocolate cream, roughly
chop the LINDT EXCELLENCE chocolate. Mix
together the egg yolks and sugar. Bring the milk
and cream to the boil in a heavy-based saucepan.
Add the chopped chocolate and mix well, then add
the egg yolk and sugar mixture. Mix well.
2. Preheat the oven to 90°C (190°F/Gas ¼).
Divide the chocolate cream between 8 individual
flameproof ramekins. Bake for 45 minutes.
3. Leave to cool, then refrigerate overnight.
4. The following day, heat the grill/broiler. Sprinkle
the crèmes brûlées with demerara/turbinado sugar
and put under the grill/broiler for 1 or 2 minutes
to caramelize the tops. Serve immediately.

Chocolate liégeois

Serves 6
Preparation time: 15 min plus chilling time
Cooking time: approx 5 min

1.2 litres (5 cups) water • 100 g (½ cup) caster/
superfine sugar • 250 g (9 oz) LINDT EXCELLENCE
Cocoa 70% • 50 g (½ cup) cocoa powder
200 ml (¾ cup) whipping or double/heavy cream
750 ml (25 oz) chocolate ice cream • LINDT
EXCELLENCE Cocoa 70%, grated, to decorate

....

1. Put a large freezer-proof bowl in the freezer.
2. Meanwhile, prepare the chocolate drink. Bring
the water to the boil in a saucepan with the sugar.
Roughly chop the LINDT EXCELLENCE chocolate,
then add to the boiling water with the cocoa
powder, beating vigorously all the time. Bring the
mixture back to the boil, then remove from the heat.
3. Beat for 3 minutes more, then put in a large bowl.
Leave to cool, then refrigerate until the chocolate
drink is completely chilled.
4. Remove the bowl from the freezer and pour in the
cream. Beat the cream to form stiff peaks. Put the
whipped cream into a piping bag fitted with a fluted
nozzle/tip.
5. To serve, put 2 scoops of chocolate ice cream
per person at the bottom of each tall glass. Pour
the chilled chocolate drink on top, and top with the
whipped cream. Sprinkle with the grated chocolate
and serve immediately.

Chocolate–vanilla bavarois

Serves 4–6
Preparation time: 1 hr
Chilling time: 6 hr

350 ml (1½ cups) prepared custard • 3 leaves of gelatine • 300 ml (1¼ cups) whipping or double/heavy cream, chilled • 70 ml (⅓ cup) whole milk, chilled • 70 g (2½ oz) LINDT EXCELLENCE Cocoa 70% • 2 tsp vanilla essence • sunflower oil, for greasing

....

1. Gently heat the custard in a heavy-based saucepan, then pour it into a bowl. Soften the gelatine in a bowl of cold water, then squeeze out the excess water. Add the squeezed-out gelatine to the warm custard and stir to dissolve.
2. Plunge the bowl of custard into a bowl of ice cubes and stir until the custard starts to thicken. Mix together the cream and milk and beat to form stiff peaks. Stir the whipped cream into the custard to make the bavarois mixture.
3. Divide the bavarois mixture in half.
4. Break the LINDT EXCELLENCE chocolate into pieces and melt it in a bowl in a bain-marie. Mix the melted chocolate into one half of the bavarois mixture and add the vanilla essence to the other half.
5. Grease a 22-cm (8½-in) diameter springform tin/pan. Pour in the chocolate bavarois mixture, then refrigerate for 30 minutes until the mixture becomes firm.
6. Pour the vanilla bavarois mixture on top. Refrigerate for 4–5 hours more until the bavarois is completely firm.
7. Turn the bavarois out and serve immediately.

Tip! Dip the springform tin/pan in hot water for a few moments to make it easier to turn the bavarois out.

Chocolate macaroons

Makes approx 20 macaroons
Preparation time: 25 min
Cooking time: 20–25 min

For the ganache: 175 g (6 oz) LINDT EXCELLENCE
Cocoa 70% • 300 ml (1¼ cups) whipping
or double/heavy cream
For the macaroons: 220 g (1¾ cups) icing/
confectioner's sugar • 120 g (1½ cups) ground
almonds • 4 egg whites, chilled overnight
50 g (¼ cup) caster/superfine sugar
30 g (⅓ cup) cocoa powder

. . . .

1. Prepare the ganache. Break the LINDT
EXCELLENCE chocolate into pieces and melt it
in a bowl in a bain-marie. Add the cream and mix
with a spatula until smooth and creamy. Set aside.
2. Prepare the macaroons. Preheat the oven to
160°C (325°F/Gas 3). Mix together the icing/
confectioner's sugar and ground almonds and
spread on a baking sheet. Bake for 5–10 minutes.
3. In a large bowl, beat the egg whites until stiff.
Gradually add the caster/superfine sugar, beating
all the time. Gently fold in the cocoa powder and the
sugar and almond mixture.
4. Fill a piping bag fitted with a plain nozzle/tip with
the mixture. Pipe evenly sized circles onto a baking
sheet lined with baking parchment. Set aside for 20
minutes, then bake for 12–15 minutes.
5. Remove from the oven and leave to cool slightly.
Trickle some water between the parchment and the
baking sheet; this will create a little steam, which will
make it easier to remove the macaroons.
6. Stir the ganache a little, then use a spatula to
sandwich the macaroons in pairs with the ganache.

Tip: Store the macaroons in a cool place.

Chocolate-coffee tartlets

Serves 4–6
Preparation time: 25 min
Cooking time: approx 30 min

1 knob of unsalted butter, for greasing • 320 g (11 oz) sweet shortcrust pastry (bought or home-made) • 200 ml (¾ cup) whipping or double/heavy cream • 80 g (3 oz) LINDT EXCELLENCE Cocoa 70% • 50 ml (¼ cup) strong coffee • ½ tsp coffee extract • 1 egg

....

1. Preheat the oven to 190°C (375°F/Gas 5). Butter 4–6 individual tart tins. Roll out the shortcrust pastry and use to line the tins. Bake blind for 5–7 minutes. Remove from the oven.

2. Bring the cream to the boil in a heavy-based saucepan. Remove from the heat. Break the LINDT EXCELLENCE chocolate into pieces and add. Beat well until smooth and creamy.

3. In a large bowl, beat together the coffee, coffee extract and egg. Add the cream and chocolate mixture, stir well, then pour into the pastry cases and put in the oven.

4. Turn off the oven and leave the tartlets there for about 20 minutes until the chocolate mixture has become firm. Remove from the oven and leave to cool slightly. Serve immediately.

Excellent idea! To enjoy the flavour of these tartlets at its best, eat them as soon as possible after removing from the oven.

Mini chocolate-caramel slices

Serves 4
Preparation time: 20 min
Freezing time: 6 hr minimum

Approx 10 digestive biscuits/graham crackers
90 g (⅓ cup) dulce de leche • 350 g (12 oz) LINDT
EXCELLENCE Cocoa 70% • 125 g (1 stick) slightly
salted butter • 125 g (1 cup) icing/
confectioner's sugar

....

1. Line 4 mini loaf tins/pans with cling film/plastic
wrap. Crush the biscuits/crackers and set aside.
2. Gently heat the dulce de leche until it liquefies.
Set aside.
3. Break the LINDT EXCELLENCE chocolate into
pieces and melt it in a bowl in a bain-marie. Add
the butter and icing/confectioner's sugar, and stir
with a spatula until smooth and creamy.
4. One-third fill the prepared mini loaf tins/pans with
the chocolate mixture, then sprinkle with some of the
crushed biscuits/crackers. Pour over the liquefied
dulce de leche, add another layer of crushed
biscuits/crackers, and finish with a second layer
of chocolate mixture.
5. Freeze the mini-slices for at least 6 hours. Remove
from the freezer 15 minutes before serving.

Excellent idea! If you want your mini-slices to be
more crunchy, add some chopped hazelnuts to the
chocolate mixture.

Rose-leaf biscuits

Makes 45–50 biscuits/cookies
Preparation time: 40 min
Cooking time: 8–10 min
Chilling time: 30 min

225 g (1¾ cups) plain/all-purpose flour • 1½ tbsp
unsweetened cocoa powder • 1tsp baking powder
1 pinch of salt • 150 g (¾ cup) caster/superfine
sugar • 125 g (1 stick) unsalted butter • 1 egg
150 g (5 oz) LINDT EXCELLENCE Cocoa 70%
45–50 unsprayed rose leaves

....

1. Line two baking sheets with baking parchment.
Sieve the flour, cocoa powder, baking powder and
salt into a large bowl. In another bowl, beat together
the sugar and butter until pale in colour. Add the
egg and beat again.
2. Combine the two mixtures together to make a
slightly stiff dough. Divide the dough in half and
make each half into a roll 4 cm (1½in) in diameter.
3. Wrap in clingfilm/plastic wrap and put in the
fridge to chill for 30 minutes.
4. Preheat the oven to 200°C (400°F/Gas 6). Cut
the rolls of dough into circles 5 mm (¼ in) thick. Bake
in the preheated oven for 8–10 minutes, until firm but
not hard. Remove from the oven and leave to cool.
5. Meanwhile, break the LINDT EXCELLENCE
chocolate into pieces and melt it in a bowl in a
bain-marie. Brush the melted chocolate over the top
of the rose leaves, setting aside a small amount of
chocolate. When the chocolate has set, carefully
peel the leaves away. Using a dab of the remaining
melted chocolate, stick one chocolate leaf on top of
each biscuit/cookie.

Excellent idea! Serve these biscuits/cookies at tea
time, or accompanied by some vanilla or chocolate
ice cream, or with a cup of hot chocolate.

Chocolate banoffee pie

Serves 6
Preparation time: 20 min
Chilling time: 1 hr 30 min

60 g (2 oz) LINDT EXCELLENCE Cocoa 70%
70 g (5 tbsp) slightly salted butter • approx 20
digestive biscuits/graham crackers • 2 bananas
5 tbsp dulce de leche • 200 ml (¾ cup) whipping
or double/heavy cream, chilled • 2 heaped tsp
vanilla sugar • 100 g (scant ½ cup) mascarpone
cocoa powder, to decorate

. . . .

1. Roughly chop the LINDT EXCELLENCE chocolate
and butter into small pieces. Melt them in a bowl in
a bain-marie and stir with a spatula until smooth and
creamy. Crush the biscuits/crackers and add to the
chocolate and butter mixture.
2. Spread the mixture in the bottom of a 22-cm
(8½-in) diameter springform tin/pan and refrigerate
for 30 minutes.
3. Cut the bananas into rounds and spread on top
of the chilled mixture in the tin. Spread with the dulce
de leche.
4. Beat the cream to form soft peaks. When the
cream starts to thicken, add the vanilla sugar and
mascarpone. Continue beating until smooth. Cover
with the cream and mascarpone mixture and
refrigerate for 1 hour.
5. Remove from the tin/pan and sprinkle with cocoa
powder. Serve immediately.

Excellent idea! A chocolate version of the classic
banoffee pie. What could be more delicious?

Dark chocolate truffles

Makes approx 20 truffles
Preparation time: 30 min
Chilling time: 2 hr

300 g (11 oz) LINDT EXCELLENCE Cocoa 70%
1 tbsp whole milk • 100 g (7 tbsp) unsalted butter
2 egg yolks • 50 ml (¼ cup) whipping or double/
heavy cream • 125 g (1 cup) icing/confectioner's
sugar • 1 tbsp rum, brandy or other spirits (optional)
250 g (2 cups) unsweetened cocoa powder

....

1. Break the LINDT EXCELLENCE chocolate into pieces and put in a bowl in a bain-marie. Add the milk and stir until smooth and creamy.
2. Gradually add the butter, a little at a time. Add the egg yolks, one at a time, followed by the cream and icing/confectioner's sugar. If desired, you can add 1 tbsp rum, brandy or other spirits. Beat the mixture well for 5 minutes.
3. Spread the mixture to a thickness of roughly 2 cm (¾ in) onto a baking sheet lined with baking parchment. Refrigerate for 2 hours.
4. Cut the chilled mixture into small squares. Put the cocoa powder in a shallow dish, dip your fingers in the cocoa and quickly roll each square of chocolate into a ball between your fingers. Put each coated truffle back in the cocoa as you go. Work fast so the truffles don't become soft.
5. When all the truffles are finished, remove from the cocoa powder.

Tip! Keep the truffles cool (but not in the fridge) until ready to serve.

Old-fashioned hot chocolate drink

Serves 4
Preparation time: 15 min

125 g (4 oz) LINDT EXCELLENCE Cocoa 70%
500 ml (2 cups) mineral water • 50 g (¼ cup)
caster/superfine sugar • 25 g (¼ cup) cocoa powder

....

1. Break the LINDT EXCELLENCE chocolate into pieces and put in a large bowl.
2. Bring the water to the boil in a saucepan with the sugar. Add the cocoa powder and beat together vigorously. Bring back to the boil, then remove from the heat.
3. Pour one-third of the sugar and cocoa powder solution at a time over the pieces of chocolate. Mix gently using a wooden spoon, starting from the centre and working outwards.
4. Beat for 5 minutes using an electric hand-held mixer. Divide the hot chocolate between 4 cups and serve immediately.

Excellent idea! This smooth, creamy hot chocolate is delicious on its own or accompanied by a few small, plain biscuits/cookies, whatever the time of day ...

CONVERSION TABLE

Weight	55 g	100 g	150 g	200 g	250 g	300 g	500 g	750 g	1 kg
	2 oz	3½ oz	5 oz	7 oz	9 oz	11 oz	18 oz	27 oz	36 oz

These conversions are correct to within a few grams (1 oz actually equals 28 g).

Volume	15 ml	50 ml	100 ml	250 ml	500 ml	750 ml	1 litre
	1 tbsp	¼ cup	scant ½ cup	1 cup	2 cups	3 cups	4 cups

To simplify measuring volume, here 1 cup is equivalent to 250 ml (1 cup actually equals 230 ml).

Photo credits

Ph © C. Faccioli (styling by C. Jausserand) p. 43

Ph E. Fénot © coll. Larousse (styling by D. Brunet) p. 35

Ph M. Pessina © coll. Larousse (styling by R. de Magistris) p. 27

Ph O. Ploton © coll. Larousse (styling by B. Abraham) pp. 5, 9, 11, 13, 15, 23,
29, 31, 33, 37, 39, 41, 47, 49, 53

Ph O. Ploton © coll. Larousse (styling by N. André) pp. 7, 19, 21, 25, 51, 53

Ph P-L Viel © coll. Larousse (styling by V. Drouet) pp. 17, 45

Colour reproduction: Turquoise, Émerainville
Printed in China by Leo Paper Products